All About Cake Pop

Learn How to Make Fun and Delicious Cake Pops at Home!

BY: Valeria Ray

License Notes

Table of Contents

Introduction 6

1) Chocolate Cake Pops 7

2) Pumpkin & Pecan Cake Pops 10

3) Cinnamon Cake Pops 12

4) Maple & Bacon Cake Pops 14

5) Cake Batter Cake Pops 17

6) Marshmallow Cake Pops 19

7) Salted Caramel Cake Pops 21

8) Strawberry Truffle Cake Pops 23

9) German Chocolate Cake Pops 25

10) Vanilla Cake Pops 27

11) Cherry and Vanilla Cake Pops 29

12) Caramel Walnut Cake Pops 31

13) Coconut Cake Pops 33

14) Coffee Chocolate Cake Pops 35

15) Pecan Pie Cake Pops 37

16) Red Velvet Cake Pops 39

17) Peanut Butter Cake Pops 41

18) Yellow-Cake Cake Pops 43

19) Snowman Cake Pops 45

20) Coconut Caramel Cake Pops 47

21) Oatmeal Crème Pie Cake Pops 49

22) Key Lime Pie Cake Pops 51

23) Peppermint Cake Pops 53

24) Chocolate-Fudge Cake Balls 55

25) Red Velvet Cheesecake Cake Balls 58

26) Strawberry Shortcake Cake Pops 61

27) Vanilla & Peppermint Cake Pops 63

28) Lemon Cake Pops 65

29) Corn Dog Cake Pop 67

30) Funfetti Cake Pops 70

Conclusion 72

About the Author.. 73

Author's Afterthoughts.. 74

Introduction

Sick of cakes and cupcakes? Cake pops are what you need! Cake pops are a yummy bite-sized delight and are cute and fancy at the same time, which makes them perfect for weddings, parties, brunches, and a lot more.

This recipe book boasts flavors ranging from vanilla chocolate, and coconut to maple, pecan, and peanut butter, this recipe book has something for everyone.

So, what are you waiting for? Choose a recipe and let's get going!

1) Chocolate Cake Pops

Delicious classic chocolate-covered cake pop recipe!

Makes: 96 cake pops

Prep: 25 mins

Bake: 20 mins

Ingredients:

- 1 pack of regular size devil's food cake mix
- 1 cup of chocolate fudge frosting
- 1 tsp. of instant coffee granules
- ⅓ cup of baking cocoa
- 1 ⅓ cups of miniature semisweet chocolate chips
- 2 lb. of chopped white candy coating
- ¼ cup of chocolate syrup
- 2 tbsp. of hot water
- Optional: toasted sweetened shredded coconut, crushed candy canes, and milk chocolate English toffee bits

Directions:

Prepare & bake the cake according to the package instructions.

Let it cool completely and crumble in a large bowl.

Mix the water and coffee granules in a small bowl until it is dissolved.

Stir in the cocoa, chocolate syrup, and frosting.

Add to the cake and beat using a low speed until it is blended. Stir the chocolate chips.

Shape the mixture into 1-inch balls.

Melt the candy coating in a microwave and stir until it becomes smooth.

Dip the balls in the melted coating and let the excess drip.

Put them on waxed paper and put your chosen toppings. Let it stand until it becomes set.

2) Pumpkin & Pecan Cake Pops

This cake pop recipe is best made in the fall or for the Thanksgiving celebration.

Makes: 35 cake pops

Prep: 2 hrs. 10 mins

Bake: -

Ingredients:

- 2 pumpkin-flavored 8- or 9-inch baked cake layers
- 2 bags of white candy melts
- ¼ to ½ cup of store-bought or homemade frosting
- 1 cup of finely chopped pecans

Directions:

Crumble the cake with a fork.

Mix the frosting until the cake holds together and shape it into balls.

Put the cake balls in the freezer for 1 hr. or in the refrigerator for 2 hours.

Melt a few candy melts following the package instructions.

Dip the lollipop sticks in the candy melt mixture and insert a cake ball. Do the same for the remaining balls.

Chill for around 15 minutes or until the candy becomes hard.

Put the remaining candy melts in a small bowl and melt. Put the pecans in a different bowl.

Coat the cake pop in the candy melt mixture and tap to remove excess candy if needed. Then, dip the cake into the pecans.

Place the cake pop on a plate pecan-side down. Do the same for the remaining cake pops.

Chill until they are ready to serve.

3) Cinnamon Cake Pops

This cake pop recipe is the easiest and most kid-friendly breakfast you will make.

Makes: 13 servings

Prep: 2 hrs.

Bake: 20 mins

Ingredients:

- 1 pack of softened cream cheese
- 8 oz. of white chocolate baking squares or bars (broken into pieces)
- Optional: cinnamon sugar
- 1 can of refrigerated cinnamon rolls with icing

Directions:

Bake cinnamon rolls following the package instructions. Set aside the icing to allow it to cool for 30 minutes.

Put the cinnamon rolls in a food processor and pulse until crumbs are formed. Transfer them to a large bowl.

Mix the icing and cream cheese and knead.

Using a cookie scooper, scoop out some balls and roll them using your hands. Put the balls on a pan with baking paper.

Place the white chocolate in a small microwavable bowl, microwave on high for 1 minute, and stir. Do this repeatedly until the chocolate becomes smooth.

Dip the balls into the melted white chocolate making sure that they are evenly coated.

Put them back on the cookie sheet & sprinkle some cinnamon sugar if you want.

Let it sit for 1 to 2 hours before serving.

4) Maple & Bacon Cake Pops

The blend of bacon, walnuts, and cream cheese makes this recipe the ideal dessert for any crowd.

Makes: 48 cake pops

Prep: 25 mins

Bake: 20 mins

Ingredients:

- 10 slices of crispy cooked and crumbled precooked bacon
- 1 pack of vanilla cake mix
- 3 ½ tsp. of maple flavor
- 1 tbsp. of real maple syrup
- 2 cups of chopped walnuts
- ⅔ cup of cream cheese frosting
- ¾ cup of sugar
- 2 containers of cream cheese frosting

Directions:

Heat oven to 350 degrees.

Coat a 13x9 inch pan using cooking spray.

Prepare the cake mix as per to the instructions on package and add the bacon, 2 ½ tsp maple flavor, and 1 ¼ cups of the walnuts.

Put the mixture into the pan and bake. Allow it to cool.

Line the cookie sheet with wax paper.

Crumble the cake into a large bowl.

Combine ⅔ cup of frosting and syrup.

Shape the mixture into bowls and place it on the cookie sheet. Then freeze or refrigerate.

Cook sugar in a 12-inch skillet on medium heat. Constantly stir until it becomes golden and melted.

Add the remaining walnuts to the sugar mixture and coat them. Allow it to cool.

Put the frosting in a large microwavable bowl and microwave on medium for 30 seconds or until it becomes smooth.

Add a tsp of maple flavor.

Put the end of one stick in the frosting mixture and insert a cake ball.

Dip the cake ball into the melted frosting and drip any excess.

Place sugared nuts on top if you want.

5) Cake Batter Cake Pops

These cake balls are the same as a funfetti cake, but they are more fun!

Makes: 24 cake pops

Prep: 25 mins

Bake: 20 mins

Ingredients:

- 1 pack of funfetti cake mix
- 1 pack of white chocolate chips
- 2 tbsp. of butter
- 1 tub of vanilla or funfetti frosting
- Optional: sprinkles

Directions:

Bake the cake following the package instructions and allow it to cool.

Crumble the cake and put it in a large bowl. Add a cup of frosting & mix well.

Shape into 1-inch balls & place them on a baking tray lined with parchment paper. Freeze for 15 minutes.

Put the butter and chocolate chips in a separate bowl. Microwave in intervals and stir until it becomes smooth.

Coat the balls using the chocolate mixture and top with sprinkles.

Freeze for 5 minutes more and serve.

6) Marshmallow Cake Pops

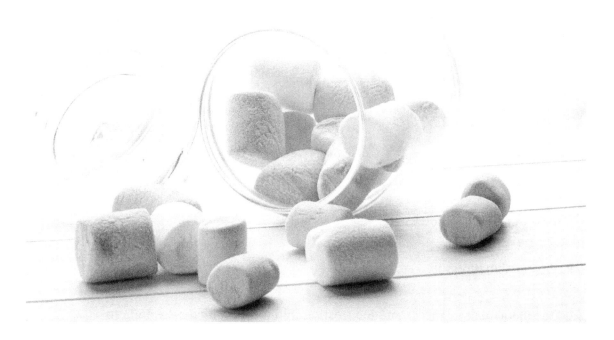

Delicious marshmallow cake pops with candy melts!

Makes: 30 cake pops

Prep: 25 mins

Bake: 20 mins

Ingredients:

- 1 pack of chocolate cake mix
- 2 bags of candy melts
- 6 pieces of big marshmallows (e.g. PEEPS)
- 1 container of chocolate frosting
- Optional: sprinkles or crushed candy canes

Procedure:

Prepare the cake as per the instructions and allow it to cool.

Crumble the cake in a bowl.

Cut the marshmallows into small pieces.

Add the marshmallow pieces and the frosting into the crumbled cake and mix.

Shape the mixture into 1-inch balls.

Melt 15 candy melts and dip the end of the lollipop sticks in the candy melt mixture. Then, insert the cake balls.

Put in the freezer for 30 mins - 1 hour.

Melt the remaining candy melts in a bowl and dip the cake pops.

Using Styrofoam, stick the opposite end of the lollipop sticks there to let the candy coating harden.

Add sprinkles/crushed candy canes on top if you want.

7) Salted Caramel Cake Pops

This cake pop combines caramel cake crumbs and salted caramel sauce.

Makes: 30 cake pops

Prep: 25 mins

Bake: 20 mins

Ingredients:

- 1 pack of caramel cake mix

For the salted caramel sauce:

- ¼ cup butter
- ¼ cup milk/cream
- ½ cup pf brown sugar
- 1 to 2 tsp. of salt
- 2 cups of melted dark chocolate

Procedure:

Prepare the cake following the package instructions. Allow it to cool.

Crumble the cake in a large bowl. Set aside

For the caramel sauce, heat the brown sugar and butter in a saucepan on medium to high heat. Then, boil for 2 mins and remove from heat.

Add salt and let it cool.

Mix the crumbled cake and caramel sauce.

Roll mixture into balls & put them in the refrigerator for about an hour.

Dip the cake balls into the melted chocolate and put them again in the refrigerator for another hour to set.

8) Strawberry Truffle Cake Pops

The rich chocolate and the hint of strawberry essence will make everyone enjoy this elegant cake pop recipe.

Makes: 30 cake pops

Prep: 25 mins

Bake: 20 mins

Ingredients:

- 1 pack of white cake mix
- ½ cup of canned vanilla frosting
- 1 tbsp. of strawberry essence
- 2 ½ lb. of chopped dark chocolate candy coating
- ⅓ cup of melted seedless raspberry jam
- Chopped pink candy coating
- Optional: red food coloring, pink sprinkles, and decorative sugar

Procedure:

Prepare and bake the cake following the package instructions. Allow it to cool.

Crumble the cake in a large bowl and add the jam, liqueur, frosting, and food coloring if you want. Mix them well.

Shape into 1-inch balls & put them on baking sheets.

Insert sticks and freeze for at least 2 hours or refrigerate for at least 3 hours.

Melt the dark chocolate in the microwave.

Dip the cake pops in the melted candy coating and drip the excess. Place them in a Styrofoam block to stand.

Melt the pink candy coating and drizzle them on the cake pops.

Decorate with the optional ingredients and let it stand before serving.

9) German Chocolate Cake Pops

If you want a twist on the traditional chocolate coating on your cake pops, you should try this recipe.

Makes: 30 cake pops

Prep: 25 mins

Bake: 20 mins

Ingredients:

- 1 pack of German chocolate cake mix
- 1 bar of coconut pecan frosting
- 2 packs of white chocolate or milk chocolate candy coating

Procedure:

Prepare the cake following package instructions.

Bake it in a 9x13 pan and allow it to cool.

Crumble the cake and add the frosting. Mix until blended well.

Shape them in 1 1/2 -inch balls and refrigerate until they become firm.

Melt the candy coating following the package instructions.

Coat the cake balls until they are covered.

Put the cake balls in the refrigerator until the coating is set.

10) Vanilla Cake Pops

Delicious vanilla cake pops that are super moist easy to make!

Makes: 30 cake pops

Prep: 25 mins

Bake: 20 mins

Ingredients:

- ¾ cup of all-purpose flour
- 3 tbsp. of vegetable oil
- ½ cup of white sugar
- ¼ tsp. of baking powder
- ¼ tsp. of salt
- ¼ cup of buttermilk
- ½ tsp. of baking soda
- 1 egg
- ½ tsp. of vanilla extract

Procedure:

Preheat your cake pop maker and put in some oil.

Combine the sugar, baking soda, baking powder, salt, and flour in a bowl.

Using an electric mixer, beat the vegetable oil, egg, vanilla extract, and buttermilk until the consistency becomes smooth.

Put 1 tbsp. of the batter in the cake pop maker.

Bake for around 4 minutes.

After removing the cake pops, allow it to cool before serving.

11) Cherry and Vanilla Cake Pops

These cake pops are not only mouth-watering but also beautiful.

Makes: 30 cake pops

Prep: 25 mins

Bake: 20 mins

Ingredients:

- 1 pack of white cake mix
- 1 cup of cream cheese frosting
- 48 drained maraschino cherries (stems removed)
- 2 to 3 tbsp. of maraschino cherry juice
- 2 ½ lb. of chopped white candy coating
- Red pearl sugar

Procedure:

Prepare and bake the cake using a greased 13x9-inch baking pan following the package instructions. Allow it to cool.

Crumble the cake in a large bowl. Add and mix the frosting and maraschino cherry juice well.

Shape the mixture into balls around the cherries and place them on baking sheets. Insert the lollipop sticks.

Freeze for at least 2 hrs. or refrigerate for at least 3 hrs.

Melt the candy coating in the microwave and stir until it becomes smooth.

Dip one cake ball in the mixture and drip the excess. Do the same for the rest of the cake mixture.

Put red pearl sugar on top and let them stand in a Styrofoam block.

12) Caramel Walnut Cake Pops

You will never go wrong with this cake pop recipe because of the delectable walnuts and buttery caramel.

Makes: 48 cake pops

Prep: 25 mins

Bake: 20 mins

Ingredients:

- 1 pack of chocolate cake mix
- ¾ cup of Dulce de leche
- 2 ½ lb. of coarsely chopped milk chocolate candy coating
- Chopped cashews

Procedure:

Prepare and bake the cake using a greased 13x9-inch baking pan following the package instructions. Allow it to cool.

Crumble the cake in a large bowl. Combine the Dulce de leche well.

Shape into 1-inch balls & put them on baking sheets. Insert lollipop sticks.

Freeze for at least 2 hrs. or refrigerate for at least 3 hrs.

Melt the candy coating in a microwave and stir until smooth.

Dip each ball into the coating and drip the excess.

Coat with walnuts.

Let the cake pop stands by inserting them in a Styrofoam block.

13) Coconut Cake Pops

Yummy coconut cake pops that all coconut lovers are bound to love!

Makes: 30 cake pops

Prep: 25 mins

Bake: 20 mins

Ingredients:

- ¾ cup of all-purpose flour
- ½ cup of white sugar
- ½ tsp. of baking soda
- ¼ tsp. of baking powder
- ¼ tsp. of salt
- 3 tbsp. of vegetable oil
- ¼ cup of buttermilk
- 1 egg
- ½ tsp. of vanilla extract
- ½ cup unsweetened shredded coconut

Procedure:

Preheat your cake pop maker and put in some oil.

Combine the sugar, baking soda, baking powder, salt, and flour in a bowl.

Using an electric mixer, beat the vegetable oil, egg, vanilla extract, and buttermilk until the consistency becomes smooth. Finally, add in the coconut.

Put 1 tbsp. of the batter in the cake pop maker.

Bake for around 4 minutes.

After removing the cake pops, allow it to cool before serving.

14) Coffee Chocolate Cake Pops

Delicious chocolate and coffee-infused cake pop recipe!

Makes: 96 cake pops

Prep: 25 mins

Bake: 20 mins

Ingredients:

- 1 pack of regular size devil's food cake mix
- 1 cup of chocolate fudge frosting
- 1 tbsp. of instant coffee granules
- ⅓ cup of baking cocoa
- 1 ⅓ cups of miniature semisweet chocolate chips
- 2 lb. of chopped white candy coating
- ¼ cup of chocolate syrup
- 2 tbsp. of hot water

Directions:

Prepare & bake the cake according to the package instructions.

Let it cool completely and crumble in a large bowl.

Mix the water and coffee granules in a small bowl until it is dissolved.

Stir in the cocoa, chocolate syrup, and frosting.

Add to the cake and beat using a low speed until it is blended. Stir the chocolate chips.

Shape the mixture into 1-inch balls.

Melt the candy coating in a microwave and stir until it becomes smooth.

Dip the balls in the melted coating and let the excess drip.

Put them on waxed paper and put your chosen toppings. Let it stand until it becomes set.

15) Pecan Pie Cake Pops

Delicious pecan pie cake pop recipe that's perfect for fall and winter!

Makes: 35 cake pops

Prep: 25 mins

Bake: 20 mins

Ingredients:

- 2 vanilla-flavored 8- or 9-inch baked cake layers
- 2 bags of white candy melts
- ¼ to ½ cup of store-bought or homemade frosting
- 1 cup of finely chopped pecans

Directions:

Crumble the cake using a fork.

Mix the frosting until the cake holds together and shape it into balls.

Put in the freezer for an hour or in the refrigerator for 2 hours.

Melt a few candy melts following the package instructions.

Dip the lollipop sticks in the candy melt mixture and insert a cake ball. Do the same for the remaining balls.

Chill for around 15 minutes or until the candy becomes hard.

Put the remaining candy melts in a small bowl and melt. Put the pecans in a different bowl.

Coat the cake pop in the candy melt mixture and tap to remove excess candy if needed. Then, dip the cake into the pecans.

Place the cake pop on a plate pecan-side down. Do the same for the remaining cake pops.

Chill until ready to serve.

16) Red Velvet Cake Pops

Red velvet lovers are going to love these moist and delicious cake pops!

Makes: 30 cake pops

Prep: 25 mins

Bake: 20 mins

Ingredients:

- ¾ cup of all-purpose flour
- ½ cup of white sugar
- ½ tsp. of baking soda
- ¼ tsp. of baking powder
- ¼ tsp. of salt
- 3 tbsp. of vegetable oil
- ¼ cup of buttermilk
- 1 egg
- ½ tsp. of vanilla extract
- 1 tsp red food coloring

Procedure:

Preheat your cake pop maker and put in some oil.

Combine the sugar, baking soda, baking powder, salt, and flour in a bowl.

Using an electric mixer, beat the vegetable oil, egg, vanilla extract, buttermilk, and red food coloring until the consistency becomes smooth.

Put 1 tbsp. of the batter in the cake pop maker.

Bake for around 4 minutes.

After removing the cake pops, allow it to cool before serving.

17) Peanut Butter Cake Pops

Peanut butter with vanilla frosting and delicious cake!

Makes: 30 cake pops

Prep: 25 mins

Bake: 20 mins

Ingredients:

- 1 pack of cake mix
- 2 cups of vanilla frosting
- ½ cup creamy peanut butter

Procedure:

Prepare and bake the cake using a greased 13x9-inch baking pan following the package instructions. Allow it to cool.

Crumble the cake in a bowl & mix half a cup of the frosting.

Place the cake mixture in ice cube trays made of silicone. Insert lollipop sticks.

Freeze for at least 2 hrs. or refrigerate for at least 3 hrs.

Run a small spatula around every cube to easily remove the cake pops.

Warm the remaining vanilla frosting in the microwave. Add in the creamy peanut butter and stir until smooth.

Dip the cake pops in the warmed frosting and peanut butter mixture and let them stand in a Styrofoam block.

Allow it to stand before serving.

18) Yellow-Cake Cake Pops

A basic yellow-cake cake pop recipe. You can add in any toppings you want– the possibilities are endless!

Makes: 30 cake pops

Prep: 25 mins

Bake: 20 mins

Ingredients:

- 1 pack of yellow cake mix
- 2 ½ cups of vanilla frosting
- Toppings (sprinkles, chocolate chips, M&Ms, etc.)

Procedure:

Prepare and bake the cake using a greased 13x9-inch baking pan following the package instructions. Allow it to cool.

Crumble the cake in a bowl & mix half a cup of the frosting.

Place the cake mixture in ice cube trays made of silicone. Insert lollipop sticks.

Freeze for at least 2 hrs. or refrigerate for at least 3 hrs.

Run a small spatula around every cube to easily remove the cake pops.

Warm the remaining vanilla frosting in the microwave. Stir until smooth.

Dip the cake pops in the warmed frosting and let them stand in a Styrofoam block.

Dip them in toppings once slightly cooled and allow it to stand before serving.

19) Snowman Cake Pops

These cake pops are a great and delicious way to build a snowman in your kitchen!

Makes: 30 cake pops

Prep: 25 mins

Bake: 20 mins

Ingredients:

- 1 pack of chocolate cake mix
- 2 ½ cups of cream cheese frosting
- Sprinkles, red fruit rolls and M&M's minis

Procedure:

Prepare and bake the cake using a greased 13x9-inch baking pan following the package instructions. Allow it to cool.

Crumble the cake in a bowl & mix half a cup of the frosting well.

Shape mixture into small and big balls and put them on baking sheets.

Freeze for at least 2 hrs. or refrigerate for at least 3 hrs.

To make the snowmen, insert a stick into a big cake ball and followed by a small cake ball.

Let the cake pop stands by inserting them in a foam block.

Warm the remaining frosting in a microwave and stir. Pour a spoon on each cake pop.

Add faces and buttons using sprinkles to make snowmen. Use the M&M's minis and fruit rolls for the earmuffs and scarves.

Let the snowman balls stand before serving.

20) Coconut Caramel Cake Pops

You can have your tropical escape at home when you make these cake pops.

Makes: 48 cake pops

Prep: 25 mins

Bake: 20 mins

Ingredients:

- 1 pack of angel food cake mix
- 1 cup of sweetened shredded coconut
- ¾ cup of canned vanilla frosting
- 1 tsp. of coconut extract
- ¼ cup caramel sauce
- 2 /2 lb. of melted white candy coating
- Lightly toasted sweetened shredded coconut

Procedure:

Prepare and bake the cake following the package instructions. Allow it to cool.

Add and mix the frosting, extract, caramel, and coconut in a large-sized bowl.

Crumble the cake and mix the crumbs in the frosting mixture.

Next, shape the mixture into 1-inch balls and put them on baking sheets.

Insert sticks and freeze for at least 2 hours or refrigerate for at least 3 hours.

Dip the cake pops in the melted candy coating and drip the excess.

Coat with the toasted coconut and allow to stand in a Styrofoam block before serving.

21) Oatmeal Crème Pie Cake Pops

Just 2 ingredients are all you need for this delicious make this recipe!

Makes: 48 cake pops

Prep: 25 mins

Bake: 20 mins

Ingredients:

- 12 pieces of oatmeal cream pies
- 8 oz. of white chocolate or white candy melts

Procedure:

Line a baking sheet with wax or parchment paper.

Crumble all the cream pies using a stand mixer or your hands.

Set aside ¼ cup of the crumbs.

Roll the rest of the crumbs into balls and put them on the baking sheet.

Put the balls in the refrigerator for 10 minutes.

Melt the chocolate in a bowl following the package instructions.

Coat the cake pops in the melted chocolate and put them back on the baking sheet.

Put the crumbled cream pies that you set aside.

Allow the coating to harden & serve immediately.

22) Key Lime Pie Cake Pops

This is the perfect recipe for all key lime lovers out there.

Makes: 40 servings

Prep: 25 mins

Bake: 20 mins

Ingredients:

- 1 pack of key lime cake mix
- ½ cup of key lime frosting
- 2 packs of vanilla candy coating
- Graham cracker crumbs
- 3 to 4 drops of lime oil

Procedure:

Prepare the cake as per the instructions.

Crumble the cake into a bowl, then add the frosting & mix well.

Shape them into 1-inch balls.

Place them in the refrigerator for around 1 to 2 hours.

Melt the candy coating following the package directions. Stir the lime oil in.

Dip the cake balls in the mixture & place them on was paper.

Put graham cracker crumbs on top.

23) Peppermint Cake Pops

Delicious peppermint bark cake pop recipe that's perfect for the holidays!

Makes: 40 servings

Prep: 25 mins

Bake: 20 mins

Ingredients:

- 1 9x13 baked and cooled chocolate cake
- 1 can of vanilla frosting
- 16 oz. of vanilla almond bark
- 2 tsp. of peppermint extract
- 4 crushed peppermint candy canes

Procedure:

Crumble the cake in a large bowl.

Add the frosting and mix until a dough forms.

Shape the cake mixture into balls and put them on a baking sheet with wax paper. Refrigerate for about 1 hr.

Melt the almond bark following the package instructions.

Dip the lollipop sticks in the almond bark mixture and insert the cake balls.

Put them back in the fridge until the sticks are stable in the middle of the cake balls.

Dip the cake pops in the remaining almond bark mixture and drip any excess mixture.

Sprinkle with crushed candy cane right away and place them on a baking sheet with wax paper.

Allow the cake pops to set and serve.

24) Chocolate-Fudge Cake Balls

Even though these cake balls are similar to a cake pop minus the stick, they will surely satisfy your sweet tooth.

Makes: 96 balls

Prep: 25 mins

Bake: 20 mins

Ingredients:

- 1 pack of regular size devil's food cake mix
- 1 cup of chocolate fudge frosting
- 1 tsp. of instant coffee granules
- ⅓ cup of baking cocoa
- 1 ⅓ cups of miniature semisweet chocolate chips
- 2 lb. of chopped white candy coating
- ¼ cup of chocolate syrup
- 2 tbsp. of hot water
- Optional: toasted sweetened shredded coconut, crushed candy canes, and milk chocolate English toffee bits

Directions:

Prepare & bake the cake according to the package instructions.

Let it cool completely and crumble in a large bowl.

Mix the water and coffee granules in a small bowl until it is dissolved.

Stir in the cocoa, chocolate syrup, and frosting.

Add to the cake and beat using a low speed until it is blended. Stir the chocolate chips.

Shape the mixture into 1-inch balls.

Melt the candy coating in a microwave and stir until it becomes smooth.

Dip the balls in the melted coating and let the excess drip.

Put them on waxed paper and put your chosen toppings. Let it stand until it becomes set.

25) Red Velvet Cheesecake Cake Balls

These cake balls are a bomb because of the blend of creamy cheesecake and delicious red velvet brownies.

Makes: 96 cake pops

Prep: 25 mins

Bake: 20 mins

Ingredients:

- 1 baked and cooled small cheesecake
- 2 eggs
- 1 box of red velvet mix
- 1 pack of vanilla candy coating
- ½ cup of oil
- Edible gold stars or sprinkles

Directions:

Preheat your oven to 350 degrees and use a cooking spray to grease a 13x9-inch baking pan.

Mix the eggs, cake mix, and oil in a large bowl until blended. Transfer the mixture into pan & bake for around 15 to 17 mins until the middle is set and the edges become slightly brown. Allow it to cool.

Using a cookie dough scoop, shape chunks of cheesecake into balls. Put the balls on a foil-lined baking sheet and freeze for around 2 hours or until they become firm.

Cut the cake into 1-inch squares and throw the rough edges. Flatten the squares using your palm and wrap the cheesecake balls.

Put in the freezer for around 15 mins/until they become hard.

Melt the candy coating following the package instructions.

Dip the cake balls into the candy coating and drip the excess. Then, put them back on the baking sheet.

Put the sprinkle or gold starts if you want.

26) Strawberry Shortcake Cake Pops

This cake pop recipe will be your next favorite dessert in summer.

Makes: 96 cake pops

Prep: 25 mins

Bake: 20 mins

Ingredients:

- 1 lb. of chopped strawberries
- 12 oz. of pound cake
- 12 oz. of white chocolate dripping tray
- 16 oz. of fluffy white frosting

Directions:

Crumble the pound cake in a large bowl.

Add and mix the frosting. Fold the strawberries in.

Put in the refrigerator for 30 mins.

Use wax/parchment paper to line a cookie sheet.

Shape the mixture into balls and put them on the cookie sheet. Place a stick on each ball.

Put in the freezer until they harden.

Melt the white chocolate tray for 45 seconds in the microwave. Stir and microwave until the texture becomes smooth.

Dip the balls in the tray and drip the excess.

Put the balls in the refrigerator for 1 to 3 hours and serve.

27) Vanilla & Peppermint Cake Pops

Delicious vanilla cake pops that are super moist easy to make!

Makes: 30 cake pops

Prep: 25 mins

Bake: 20 mins

Ingredients:

- ¾ cup of all-purpose flour
- ½ cup of white sugar
- ½ tsp. of baking soda
- ¼ tsp. of baking powder
- ¼ tsp. of salt
- 3 tbsp. of vegetable oil
- ¼ cup of buttermilk
- 1 egg
- ½ tsp. of peppermint extract

Directions:

Preheat your cake pop maker and put in some oil.

Combine the sugar, baking soda, baking powder, salt, and flour in a bowl.

Using an electric mixer, beat the vegetable oil, egg, peppermint extract, and buttermilk until the consistency becomes smooth.

Put 1 tbsp. of the batter in the cake pop maker.

Bake for around 4 minutes.

After removing the cake pops, allow it to cool before serving.

28) Lemon Cake Pops

This is the perfect recipe for all lemon lovers out there.

Makes: 40 cake pops

Prep: 2 hrs.

Bake: 20 mins

Ingredients:

- 1 pack of lemon cake mix
- ½ cup of lemon frosting
- 2 packs of vanilla candy coating
- Graham cracker crumbs
- 3 to 4 drops of lemon juice

Directions:

Prepare the cake mix following the package instructions.

Crumble the cake into a large bowl, add the frosting and mix well.

Shape them into 1-inch balls.

Place them in the refrigerator for around 1 to 2 hours.

Melt the candy coating following the package directions. Stir the lime oil in.

Dip the cake balls in the candy-coating mixture and place them on was paper.

Put graham cracker crumbs on top.

29) Corn Dog Cake Pop

These are cake pops that are decorated to look like corn dogs.

Makes: 40 cake pops

Prep: 45 mins

Bake: 20 mins

Ingredients:

- 1 baked yellow cake
- 2 bags of peanut butter chips
- 1 tbsp. of chocolate frosting
- ¼ to ½ cup of vanilla frosting
- 8 oz. of white chocolate candy melts or coating
- ¼ cup of graham cracker crumbs
- Yellow candy coloring

Procedure:

Crumble the yellow cake and add the chocolate and vanilla frosting. Mix well.

Scoop some of the mixtures and roll them into hotdog-shaped logs.

Put the peanut butter chips and 6 oz. of the white chocolate candy melts in a small microwavable bowl.

Microwave on high for 30 seconds and stir. Do this repeatedly until it all melts.

Add the graham cracker crumbs.

Dip the end of a lollipop stick into the candy mixture and insert a cake ball. Do the same for the rest.

Freeze the cake pops for 10 minutes

Put the peanut butter coating on every log and let the excess drip.

Melt the remaining white chocolate candy melts and mix the candy coloring. Use this to pipe on the cake pops to look like mustard.

Freeze for 2 to 3 minutes.

30) Funfetti Cake Pops

These funfetti cake balls are the same as a funfetti cake, but they are more fun. They are adorable and easy to serve.

Makes: 24 cake pops

Prep: 25 mins

Bake: 20 mins

Ingredients:

- 1 pack of funfetti cake mix
- 1 pack of white chocolate chips
- 2 tbsp. of butter
- 1 tub of vanilla or funfetti frosting
- Optional: sprinkles

Directions:

Bake the cake following the package instructions and allow it to cool.

Crumble the cake and put it in a large bowl. Add a cup of frosting and mix well.

Shape the mixture into 1-inch balls and place them on a baking tray lined with parchment paper. Freeze for 15 minutes.

Put the butter and chocolate chips in a separate bowl. Microwave in intervals and stir until it becomes smooth.

Coat the balls using the chocolate mixture and top with sprinkles.

Freeze for 5 minutes more and serve.

Conclusion

With this cookbook, you can make all sorts of fun cake pops! The delicious cross between a moist cake and sweet coating makes them delicious. Moreover, you can decorate them in various designs, making them the ideal party treat. Try all of them to find your favorite!

About the Author

A native of Indianapolis, Indiana, Valeria Ray found her passion for cooking while she was studying English Literature at Oakland City University. She decided to try a cooking course with her friends and the experience changed her forever. She enrolled at the Art Institute of Indiana which offered extensive courses in the culinary Arts. Once Ray dipped her toe in the cooking world, she never looked back.

When Valeria graduated, she worked in French restaurants in the Indianapolis area until she became the head chef at one of the 5-star establishments in the area. Valeria's attention to taste and visual detail caught the eye of a local business person who expressed an interest in publishing her recipes. Valeria began her secondary career authoring cookbooks and e-books which she tackled with as much talent and gusto as her first career. Her passion for food leaps off the page of her books which have colourful anecdotes and stunning pictures of dishes she has prepared herself.

Valeria Ray lives in Indianapolis with her husband of 15 years, Tom, her daughter, Isobel and their loveable Golden Retriever, Goldy. Valeria enjoys cooking special dishes in her large, comfortable kitchen where the family gets involved in preparing meals. This successful, dynamic chef is an inspiration to culinary students and novice cooks everywhere.

Author's Afterthoughts

Thank you for Purchasing my book and taking the time to read it from front to back. I am always grateful when a reader chooses my work and I hope you enjoyed it!

With the vast selection available online, I am touched that you chose to be purchasing my work and take valuable time out of your life to read it. My hope is that you feel you made the right decision.

I very much would like to know what you thought of the book. Please take the time to write an honest and informative review on Amazon.com. Your experience and opinions will be of great benefit to me and those readers looking to make an informed choice.

With much thanks,

Valeria Ray

Printed in Great Britain
by Amazon

26879173R00044